CU00829807

A Body Made of You

Melissa Lee-Houghton was born in Wythenshawe, Manchester in 1982. Her poetry, short fiction and reviews have been published in literary magazines such as *Succour*, *The Short Review*, *Magma* and *Tears in the Fence*. She lives in Blackburn, Lancashire.

A Body Made of
You

Melissa Lee-Houghton

Penned in the Margins
LONDON

PUBLISHED BY PENNED IN THE MARGINS
53 Arcadia Court, 45 Old Castle Street, London E1 7NY
www.pennedinthemargins.co.uk

First published 2011

ISBN
978-1-908058-00-3

AUTHOR'S NOTE

This is a selection of poems written for other writers, artists, strangers, lovers and friends.

Thank you to all the sitters for allowing me to write their portraits.

ACKNOWLEDGEMENTS

I am grateful to the editors of *Poetry Salzburg Review* and *Tears in the Fence*, in which poems from this book have appeared.

CONTENTS

To Steven

A Body Made of You

King-mask

There's room for carelessness; bodies
thrown like Jekyll's teeth.
There are bones stuck in, boners
that never came and your name
screwed in a letter.
I'd wire it to a bomb.
Age hasn't aged you but I fear
your body over the back of a chair,
a rat nibbling your ear. Will you
be announced, to me?   I came
from Hades, waltzing black, for irony.
I couldn't stand the sound of lyres or
loves — we ate steak but what we needed
was blood; you are halfways
pure alcohol, chemical — you strut
like a wary, wily, thirsty cat in a desert and all of your
prey circle you while you hold the chewed pencil
to Judas — draw a fucking star, a bent halo; Osiris —
I will put stars all around your poorly head,
I will mould them with my hands —
and like Tom and Jerry you will go soft
when your clothes fall off and there is no chase,
no whirring of canaries around your cerebellum —

opportunities should never be missed
while there is
still time for adulteries.
All the true gods mastered this.

Dog-mask

As Goya held fast to
what death is to madness then
so you are to flesh.

You fear the moon,
the shy girl in the studio.
She does not ask for sex but shows

carnage in her liquid eyes. She looks toward the bed.
You cut her with the edge of a brush, a lick —
wanting to devour her, unsettle

her to goose-pimples.
She keeps her shoulders shrugged and tense; oh
the work involved to loosen them.

I envy that you've lived your visions out
in paint, in bedsheets, having discerned a normality
of Being, a pure boredom

of suffering expectancy, acceptance and awe.
You're white as wood and dark
as a mouthful of bitter liquorice-spit.

When I called to you days ago
you just answered, but my dear you are down

and have always been down that well, and have severed

your own ropes, broken your own wiry spine
(*while I was building a stretcher from rusted iron,
casting a real dead head in bronze, you understand*) —

but dear friend, your skin looks tired with bruises
around the eyes; where I too have lost all tenderness.
You let my difficult whispers coil

in your frontal lobes. De-structured,
I give you handfuls of glass, a glass full of blood,
a sterile wish for silence

or a mask with dog teeth
to put on a face that women won't want then
to sit in your lap and be rocked like back when

you were king of tides and waves of orgasms.
I will ask you to wear your mask, like me,
and I'll keep my dress on and my sensible shoes.

But I imagine first that you will catch your real face
in one of those mirrors I should've smashed —
and then I just know that you'd cut off your nose.

Straight Faced

Wolves, fur the colour of liquor kegs,
lean every muscle into their haunches, licking
the milk out of the children's bowls and the coffee
from my cups, ripping out raincoats and snowcoats
and hats from the cupboard. I sit still at the end
of the room with my dressing gown on, open,
my nerves tied like a device
to my thigh. I'm menstruating —
the wolves smell me and I do not move
an inch either way or turn my face from the light.
I seem to be commanding respect and so I tell my thoughts this:
I am the stronger, I can survive without being stripped
to raw meat; a ribcage *Baby* will have to throw out with the rubbish.

I'm in the local papers in the weeks that follow;
you begin to wear a hat, you begin to care about rain
and how you answer the telephone. You've read the story
(of course everyone has) of how I rid us of wolves
by reciting incantations, by armed combat, by psychic contact —
but we all know I only grabbed
the honey pot and the fresh cooked bacon and threw them
into the next room sensing that what they craved was hot and
                                        sweet.
It was easy to shut the door, jamb the lock,
run out the back door, my hair like white fire
to tell children everywhere.

I was offered money for interviews, stories;
artists wanted to replicate the scene for photographs.
Only my hair would be neon and they'd use
trained dogs. I often wish the wolves
would come back and make my life more difficult,
because I fear I'll have no fear left
and I know I can't love without fear.

Tonight it is raining hard on your roof. I shake
all the while I wait, to turn a page, to cook a meal, to expect you —
and so you drive to our house, where the children are oblivious
and do not care why you're here. My husband also
keeps very quiet but smiles and listens, as is his nature,
even when Elizabeth pours cool milk into my hand
and he bends to lap and lap at it, and you are horrified.
When you all come closer to me you smell
        the scent of pain,
and you think of nothing else for all hours
than those wolves I bribed with sweet things —
even though flesh alone would fill them.

Portrait: Scorched and Flayed

curt throat razor muck
nick of an eyelash grey feather tip
cut with buck rage, missed like
frog hearts the gloat beat
fit angular cheekbone ripe like
ash colours, of abuses —
in the paintings there's hardness,
the jib of a coathanger, the spit
of a demon, if that is your thing-
make my legs hurt
grit jaw fence jumper
in cotton, black as state — the horse head
in the bathroom with the bottle of shells
Proust drama eater skin like matt
white of a fried egg, 1972 —
glazed with thoughts of a
suntan, Egypt, disappointment
claustrophobic pyramids, sphinxes
not for me
your thoughts kempt as secrets
scurrying in decrepit chaos
glory be
your clothes are on the floor
dripping, lino, razorblades
for dragging hearts and flaying nudes;
strewn like the profile

fixed like a foxhole
tribal violence in and out of you
mute as a lollipop or the fever
in a mouth that can't talk free
can't sneak hold or
give you, sky is bold is not
just sumptuous like blue
skirts folded neat origami
and a sash on the woman, the portrait
without wrinkles or days — sky
is a colour you use for accidents —
your sitters are vain as wasps
I would like that frantic bombshell
pupils filling like inkwells
blots evening-tide wisdom
round my neck like pearls,
wedding jewels —
you procured
from wives you got
telekinesis, affectations from girls,
you got the shapes of hair
in the breath of cold morning
and the ghoul shapes —
from dad you got
a snakeskin belt that I loved
and you pinned to the wall
strobed sunlight, for catching it I guess
and the paperbacks you added up —
because my instincts

are fertile like good semen;
I've a blonde imagination;
you: withered heart plumped
back like vicarage cushion
the moments of passion
we discussed the handrails,
kneeling
you're hungrier
than retrospect of blood,
paint that's not blood-coloured —
but you make it the colour
of blood wetted, kept wet, indebted.
I write flared madrigals —
ecstasies, the familiarity
is sawdust to you, is building
stretchers and a bleeding thumb —
putrefied scarlet spills
the studio, the blue of sailing
tattoos, the women
have breasts like small
milk pans filled with hot
milk or the fatty round of cakes —
the anti-psychotics my legs
wouldn't still;
the kick-in, your worked
bones worried feet tied tight
in black laces comfortable
as cookies and I'm not
your girl scout

superheroes of sorts my fingers stiff
like book spines you've fingered
off the dust you've
touched fires it
might happen in the annexe
it's been seen/done before
you can't eliminate
the possibility of losing
major artworks there are ways
that fire can spread just
blow the fucking roof off
but not for god,
the major rationalist he was
a major player before the cosmos
gave him the worst job
séance lover your radium
hair streaks of lightning pale
as the crucified, you're rare
like hipless
sirens, smashed
ambulances, birdcages
hung from the roof on hooks —
wear a hard hat soul breaker,
when I make it,
armed and full of rioja
cheap as knickers and fairytales;
we fix the lightness
of recognition I sit
next to you on a black bed

where it's easier not to sit
for the shapes of other bodies –
your awkward triumphs of loving
raise Hell in Purgatory, Messire –
deftly, and ageing riddled
with blood and bone,
pencils are crackable wishbones,
and break, like cheap biscuits –
we're stuck like cocoons dearest,
the photocopies curl
at the edges like paper
lit by fire only it's sunlight
it's a daylight bulb it shocks
everything in the room
into submission
headless torsos hanging heads
tissues, shoes, bottles
of Teacher's and a grubby curtain
half pulled off –
addled objects making objections;
blood spatter on the face of humans
you're not psychologically intact
like a shot glass or a full set of draughts
pieces anymore, not just transparent
rounded off like firemen, sergeants
authors, cannibals
my head culls your art –
catastrophe is waiting for me
to claim the living torch

for something unbearable
you are unbearable things
and a bearable home
with the little table and the black painted
chairs that could do with
a sunflower and a madwoman —
you listen to Ian Curtis
and you are fucking with me
I know you're not blistered
with love or sacrileges
because you repaint
and the light makes less noise
is too bright for screwing up
in a corner,
no masturbation, no mother —
the house is no longer
saturated by the hues
that freaked her goose-pimpled skin,
made you praise
all the destructive forces of inhibition
because you needed them
tall like a glass of amber beer.
no suicide, no rifles, just lamplight
making the hard-set bones
kill the bedsprings

OLIVIA

Portrait of Olivia as a Mute

Fine red lace, red gauze, and rubies wrap
around your bones; your flesh is stuffed with albino bunnies'
eyes and red-tipped glass headed pins, earrings
and red leather shoelaces. Your skin is living
and filled with nerves — there's salt in it
found in dead seas and quarries, there's fossils
in your marrow and small mammals burrow
into your major organs, curl up asleep — your womb
holds a single warm pearl that has grown since your children
were born. With all these fineries, and mermaid's hair
and a jaw as tense as a fox, you cannot undress:
you are always dressed. Your voice does not know
if it is British or indeed *if*, your throat comes from the purse
of an orchid — there is a lamb's bleat in your gut
and two brides' nervous bellies in your midriff.
I would say you were from Prague, or the Northern Hemisphere,
way up where whales drive men mad with their singing —
but you are Welsh, like rarebit. Your saliva
is Dutch champagne and your heart and your arteries map
a dynasty you share with Vikings and slaves —
if your breasts are not pert like upturned teacups
or filled with cub's milk — undo your blouse one extra button
each time you dress for the evening. Have your wrinkles

blessed with holy water — wear a turban when your hair
goes truly white, or eat it and line your scalp with peacock
feathers, furs. You are the queen of a Mancunian terrace
in need of renovation. You are a vintage whore
with your rebellion of dislocated ancestry. Your blood
shifts and crinkles like royal blue taffeta; ink marks the page
where you execute your will like a doe announcing an
ox-stern mate with a single, bleary blink.

STEVEN

laid out

your foreign bread smell
boiled bagels shoulders
round like potato, oily
inner fish skin sweet yeast
burned bonfire matchwood tongue
marijuana kiss old as bees
moustache curled walrus
sarsaparilla earlobes call
like a tender drunk piss
smells of old books rub
olive oil in your skin
straight nails the pink of
teary eyes skin like fresh
paint still moist the heat
droops the eyelids summer
is tiring on your feet
tepid showers matted
eyelashes like wet dog fur
straightened out for an alien
feet like Roman tiles veins
like common worms your leg
gets lonely in bed purrs
in sleep a cat dying

happily, your violence is just
frustration at the size
of things my hands
are just smaller than yours
we smash things like we're
children, ninety percent
of your ticklish skin
is underused
by my sad wick tongue

Anniversary of Our Libido

Now we are paper,
you pull-tug my nipple
like it would break.

Your saliva's got senses
in my skin creases, the folding
of me into a tight fix.

This is not art school. We don't
aim the camera. I am not old
and you are no longer older than I.

I shriek when you come-to,
near me captain. I remember
when I didn't, my body was used for bearings, forecasts,

bullet shapes, epitaphs, homophobes,
cheap DNA. My love, I'm cured now.
I take my pink and blue tablets

and you never damaged me; those doctors
never even gave a love bite or
crushed my glasses, and love —

I am not afraid of the hurt to which
your petrified love will have to commit.

Portrait of the Husband: *The Dream*

i like to lean my face near to
the fire
where heat is pure
i like the way our life looks
in photographs
i like my own pretences and i
hate yours when i
cut your hair i remember
all the heads of hair i have loved
in my time
and you don't mind mine
as long as it doesn't curl because i
remind your mother of your ex
girlfriend
today i stopped using
punctuation
because i feel mad
you're so in control it's always
about control with you
with me
i like to make you mad enough
to crash the car your fists
throw in the
air
a boxer
we listen to our

wedding song
you hold the steering wheel
ambivalently i tell you
everything
you don't
count my pills
anymore
just
fill my prescriptions
because you're kind and you
bed-bath women who can't move and are
ashamed of their breasts
and how
they moan
they hate you
so much when you're emptying
colostomy bags
and i have to cut your hair
perfectly
because hairdressers
get too close they
give you erections i know this
because
you can't sit still when i
use the scissors
when we do things together we don't
do things together sometimes
we just do things at the
same time but you

try harder than me
at most things
you chew gum it gives me
too much saliva and
nausea i don't know
what happened
it all got out of hand
i found it all
so beautiful
you married me with
pointy shoes that made your feet look
bigger and
pearly cufflinks
and new spectacles
i wanted
nobody there that night at all i
fell off the end of the bed on my back with my
garter still on i fell
almost unconscious and cried
we were wet from
the jacuzzi we couldn't work
at breakfast there were
hangers on they were eager
to know what we wanted
to do with our life
but all we wanted to do was
get in the car and go

ELIZABETH

princess

mucus, a rumble, lungs
crackle like crisp packets
eyes shot chewing gum pink
deep in the sockets and
tears come easy the bloom
of her is reckoning out
dimensions, breasts filling
like macaroons white dusted
skin and the sun makes
freckles little chocolate
spots, hair down
to the armpits, blonde
just dying to darken —
she blooms,
syrup saliva sticks to
lollipop lips, kisses
not to be wasted on
shoulder-height boys, when shoes
with heels
are awkward but
hail you queen

anatomy (female, 9 yrs)

wheat-sheaf hair,
raw silk, knotted where these
bad blue dreams rubbed in
skin's weightless as white
boredom is your earache
conch tinnitus hot water
bottle evening pink slap tender
heat marks on your round
right cheek full of dew
pearly as wet icing
mixed with a rump drop
of girly crush blood you
wear pink is the new red you
know time intuitively, fingerprints
the nerves in your nose the
sensors in fingertips, detuned
for childhood, comedy, innocence

on your back chimp hipbones,
legs like great
horses forelegs spirited with
the sharp enthusiasm of clean rained
air you are aware dead sorry
you cared more for pretty hair
other girls' mothers in
your image scabbed knees

from space hoppers and promises
invented ball games tennis
balls smack in the perfect
cheekbone where i see him
most you don't know roots
the grey dormouse down
on the blue scalp born
in October on a Sunday silly
hours the rain came screaming
down the window the blinds
wound open you were warmer
impish, the sweet smell
of cud and my blood needling
all wrapped in cotton smell
stitching iodine gas mask
there was nothing to forgive
heels like baby mice curled
bovine lashes spinal
structure frail as flight as
bee wings you wore
yellow then when i'd
already requested a boy

mute dancer now you
are wax mannequin on stage
hip hop and mild burlesque
girls vortex hot air black
feathers round you made up
red lipstick bronzing pearls

lashes batting doll face
piano hands weak as
beating wings

Clowns

I plan to map and photograph you, and add you
to the collection of ordinary muses that are ever
offering ink — how can I stay if you mean to lay down,
recline, and not look at me, beaming,
smirking, and smear paint all over
your face and hair; chase me through rooms
with red palms — place both prints
over my breasts. I think that you are still a boy
whose appetite for kicks is immeasurably large.

There are ravens and vultures flying around
above the roof of your house.
I watch them from my window,
and you give them all pet names and feed them
meat-scraps and little bones from your palms —
then you aim and shoot at them with paintballs.

You miss. I want to know
how much you see without your glasses.
They don't squirt water or have fake eyeballs
that pop out. I will smash them under my feet. I'd like
to break them and take off my clothes so I just
seem like shapes of light, a little triangle of a pubis —

ever get nervous? Let's paint each other
in fingerprints. I'll have to drop valium first —
you concentrate on our differences, my ears
of cloth and your photographic eyes that have learned
the art of shuttering frames, closing and filling
with silent cinematography.

I'll create our similarities. If there are none,
you be a drag queen and I'll be a man, yes —
we'll shove socks in my knickers —

we go out to the bar where everyone knows
you're a clown, but nobody knows that despite
my pencilled-in beard, I'm a woman.
Your friends smoke and drink and laugh
but soon suggest you go home, get the clown-suit
back on — suspenders are tolerable but all the rabbits
you pulled out of hats have eaten the pork scratchings.

We're going to have to do
something drastic. I just can't see you
in spandex, riding the trapeze anymore.
Why, when I say take off your clothes, why do you insist
on wearing clown shoes. We're not playmates:
I am an artist. You ask, so *why can't artists laugh.*

I am lonely and infuriated for not
finding ways of making art of you and I.
You do not love what can't be made light of —

but I'm a cold mirror; you are afraid;
and when I sit still, like I did in class
you come towards, quiet, get braver, closer;
I am the kind of animal could never be tamed —
you would like to pull my hair but instead you mark
two thick black crosses on my eyelids.

Incommunicado

There were triffids in town. The grass had grown
and nobody was willing to mow it.
All you had to do was get on a plane
and tempt death not to sink it.
The peroxide in your hair
makes you incorrigible,
makes you less of a trouble to me.
When God gave us immunity he said:
you should always wear
uncomfortable shoes and have
uncomfortable plane journeys and awkward
conversations with strangers. You should support
football teams that can't win — it's called
give and take.

ANNIE

Still

You stand behind a shadow screen
lit like a moth's wing. You take off
your plain skirt, your blouse, your underwear —
and pose for me there.

I have tried to make sure the room isn't cold;
I brought a rowan tree, some old tinsel.
You can have a dab of lippy and I'll be
sensible and fair, woman to woman,

when winding a hand to manipulate the brush, the paint
to fit your shadow, that does not show
pounds and ounces, greying hairs, or a terrified pubis.
Trust me, Annie, I am not a man, and my art will not seduce you.

A Body Made of You

Since I have your permission I shall
wrap your body in
fine Egyptian linen, spin it fast
around your breasts so the curves don't
throw me. I'll dress
you in a suit that gathered
sweatshop workers' tears and mopped yours
as you lost your womanhood to poetry.
It's not even your body that interests me, Annie —
it's not the way your foot would melt into
the sand of an equator-hot beach
or how your top lip can sip gregariously on an iced martini —
and that I can imagine it.
Do you know what is more exotic —
there are women in you
who cut trousers out of wheat sacks,
darned stockings and socks while they starved
to feed their kids, who lost husbands to shell blasts.
We forget, and so, again,
I will start by undressing you
from hip to nipple and scalp
to baby-toe; wrap you in linen stained
with the sweat from my brow and scythe-chop
your hair in one fell blow —
fasten your shirt to the helm, have you
stand like a captain. I will bend down

and shine your shoe
with my bosom showing; capture you
among stacks of beer kegs, cigarettes,
your grandfather's cauliflower that you photographed,
beside some post-war porn, women in chains,
a mafia case of filthy money
stolen from purses and litres of whiskey
in hip flasks. In pulse time
your body fills with blood and I
get my shot, your image so
close to blurring.

Escapist

There are dark things, but they are hidden beneath
like roots, feelers. Put your fingers in the ground
and tug them out and hold a handful.
Smear the soil across your face and in your mouth.
When you see him, behave like a widow;
ask him to wind a wand of lipstick, red lipstick,
and slide it over your mouth, back and forth,
and confess what you found in the soil and how
it was fertile. Burial is never a good way
of hiding words God broke —
my hands are filthy, my words
clot in my throat —
but I want to walk around your house
when you're not home, and rub my makeup
on the walls and put my footprints
on the floors, walk with my head
touching the wall, my cheek, loosening mirrors —
I want to see what your face shows in the lamplight
and terrify your cat so that she claws
at me, a mass of blood and knots of Titian hair.
I was a boy once. I know you don't understand.
But if you were only a girl the world
couldn't love you enough to harvest
in you a life of daggered expressions,
tumults, tempers, that your language graces;
your tongue deliberates

disappointments and disappointments.
You can't separate them, you might as well
clap your hands when thunder comes and say
Alcatraz.

SUZY

Carbon

I do not write to you, but of you,
because the paper that we write on
is our perishable skin.

Your photograph is inky and your face
chalked in by, honestly — honesty. You are
absolutely sure and absolutely not ready

to give. Your eyes see nothing of the dark
archipelago about your head, the lies
and the whispers surely love curtails —

that swim about your teeth and the years
that make your skin warm and then less warm.
All you know is that you need someone —

what a wedding band can do for the passage
of a girl who slips out of her knickers and into
her own despair, like there's nothing there.

Rainmaking by Proxy

Girls like you and I
made rain happen, without meaning, made
rain-storms and lightning get in the way
of outdoor games.
Instead of learning to kiss pretty boys
with wispy beards and awkward, jabbing tongues,
you learned to put your smile on
straight, and white. How to *be* straight;
how to understand the complicated
ergonomics of the phallus. You learned
how to assemble yourself politely
for Lord, master, client. I wish, my darling,
we had both made more of our women —
tempted the particular tastes of more girls.
(My first was in the back of a caravan
parked in grandma's back garden — I taught her
how to come, I wasn't yet eleven.)
I did the thing the old man had spent
all those rainy afternoons doing.

GEORGE

chopsticks

my drawing of you at the piano
was my shaky right hand attempting dimensions
where my brain had given up on the mathematics
of conscience, of other humans, so all your lines
were knots, codes — and your new black hair,
your back wrought and tight,
a rope for a spine — that you would have it cut,
those screams came through each bar of Clair De Lune
a duet somewhere closer to chopsticks
when I cried and you laughed
and then we both laughed,
when the manic depressive in the corner
asked if we could play Rachmaninov

Crying

when you cry and I ask you say
shh: because once upon a time.

you have not learned about the bribes
sex will have with you;

and you are opium ready
to have someone lie on top of you

like you're the rock of Gibraltar
and fall asleep like a sea-lion.

I tell you that we are in a mental hospital
and I'm married

and there's no way —
but even Adrian thinks I am here

to be molested. It seems I should share
my flesh with those less fortunate.

I come near and make you hot chocolate
and me cappuccino from the machine

and sit sucking the froth
off my fingers with my manic mouth.

I will not make you come.
your eyes light up like telescopes,

radiating heaven. we're not functional;
and I bite my teeth straight —

though the way you stare at me
my flesh is almost falling from my body.

Miranda

And at first you see
the siren arrogance named and had
sent to the beaches to sit on rocks
and have her knickers dirtied. But arrogance
underestimated
how, doe-eyed yet nothing like
a fawn, a clam, a clamped-shut heart
with its pearl churning —
inhaling the smoke
of sailors who never saw
a single sea, who never felt the word
she branded on their back
swordfish —
she swam.
Her liver is a coral reef
that sponged up alcohol and bled it out
until it reached the skin, evaporated.
If you tied her up with seaweed
and dragged her all the way to Beachy Head
she'd laugh so hard you'd
throw yourself off. Women this dark
and full of life inspire
only one kind of hatred. I can't

stand to tell her that it's lust —
and she talks incessantly to the stars
and somehow, leftover virtue,
or sanctity, or the way they placed
the moons in space
has kept her cooled blood safe.

Broken Poem

the Dells of Demi in her backyard,
a hand-painted mural on the back wall —
toppled swings and slides and mole holes,
treasure or marbles.
the children insist on painting
in the yellow sunshine
a halcyon sky flecked with button gold —
pots and jars
old paintbrushes there's
water for sloshing
mixing never-seen-before colours
teaching alchemy,
her father taught her he
passed it to her hand and insisted

he painted her mother;
the canvas hangs in her house
now they are not together
imbibing
cold amber whiskey fumes,
letting them settle in him warm
in his lungs and bones
he folds her in gold leaf to be rubbed away
with his thumbs
and she is the nymph
they linked with love —

they never remember her birthday,
her conception was epic,
psychedelic.
she gathers evidence of things
photos that show
frozen faces, clothes (hung like a museum
of alter-egos)

took my dress off in her room,
handprints and drawings
papers, rizlas
scribbling and books
on witchcraft and science fiction, sad novels
some poems
bras
memos

and then her grand easel as tall
and stiff as a starved soldier
holding on her stretchers

a lean-to back.

she makes portraits
of strange women for their stranger lovers
we all live
disconsolately in the past
if only someone had learned how to force her

by the shoulders
drink in that coursing deliverance
of lava —
inside there's a river
of sweet magenta that spills to your tongue

i have not forgotten the shape of her body

how we have changed since the babies came
there was
brandy on my lips
she danced heady
perspiring pure rose oil and all the
bath steam that collected in her hair
as dusk set in

the first baby
was a slipknot hiding in the crux
of her back
setting her on edge
like a panic attack until it
grew and so she
succumbed to the changes she would
have to go through —

we were only young

i was only ever
shades of Picasso-blue,

terrified of land and sea
and of pretty women −
we braved
King Arthur's palace
the tides smashed into the caves

you don't need someone to watch you dance
toward Carthage
where we will all be sitting by the beach
with our shoulders showing
little peach strap marks
where the halter-neck rests −
she will have all the worshippers
worshipping and all the dancers dancing
and the manic depressives talking and talking and her
husband will be behind the camera
taking images of her
to help in the latest application
for sainthood

and she swings in her French knickers
around the silver pole, swinging heavy and slow
closer to god
and upside down she'll go
forgetting the sky

her daddy gave her
the big red heart of a painter
and it makes mine less blue,

her brother bought me
a sari covered with
empires of stars

when i was broken
yes, love flayed our nerves,
made us sensitive —

i like it when she
wears crimson
no padding in her bra
no eyeliner just
her flame-red daughters
flopping in her lap like puppies
in the low chair

JONATHAN

Portrait of the Man as a Warm Body

Your face is civilised, like Plaster of Paris, and your mouth
is a strawberry, dying to shrink. Your blood is descended
from bears and lions. Your bones were built from fossils, the fossils
of the sea, of whales, and whale song reaches you through forests
as though your ears were attuned to only the big sounds, echoes —
the hugeness of things. Your feet were built last, from man-made
materials, from concrete blocks, and the mafia watched
as Jesus raised you, crafted and chipped your toes.
Your mother and father drew vials of blood
from hardened embers where the dinosaurs fossilised
and gave you thighs like a Roman, to make sure
you would not fall at Pilate's feet. They picked new berries
for your eyes and stole oyster pearls for your teeth,
gave you the flayed tongue of a martyr to remind you
of the importance of being quiet and sharp.
On the last day, a skin was stretched for you
from the bellies of all creatures, and made white
by the spiritual alchemy of a progressive British scientist.
The grey matter in your brain was flushed with rainwater and holy
water, and you cried when they snapped your feet and held you
like a fisherman's catch. All the dust fell off you and devoted
eyes smoothed off the rough edges and wept with joy
at the piety of you; the effable creature with blue blood

thicker than magma and ready as gunpowder
to kick-start, to give you a Greenwich pulse and a map
of the world and the determined imagination of an English explorer
waiting an age for the deep sky to open and roll thunder.

David

Players

This is our death-room.
I have asked to share this room with you.
The room is homely. There are photographs
of your friends and their friends and your parents.
There is fresh coffee brewing
and when we close our eyes we see troughs
full of milk with our faces pushed in them
and the room is built of
rusted sheet metal.
We wait for death
very calmly, on chintz sofas, and share stories.
We remember people who died before us
and we regress into belief systems
that died in childhood.
Our grandparents are waiting at the pearly gates,
sipping tea and smoking cigarettes,
handing out digestive biscuits.
It's so easy we might as well have sex,
might as well hurt each other.
If it doesn't matter, if it doesn't affect
anyone else — we could manipulate
each other into confessing what would
be taken to the grave. Hell, we might as well

love each other.
Of course, there is music
that doesn't offend. It is not
the music we would have chosen.
We are wearing comfortable clothes
but they are not the clothes we look our best in.
And there's no point in being sad,
though we are.
If death were kind this would be
a dark harem of exotic, well-read women
but for all our lifetime's wondering
it seems that death pulls us toward
strangeness and banality, and the ground,
and takes away the sky
despite the exquisite Aertex ceiling in its place
with battery-powered spotlighting.
If only death had given us
familiar things like books and songs we know
to pass the time less anxiously
forgetting our concept of Hell
and living with everyday damnation — you
boil the kettle and we decide it's time
to ask one another's forgiveness for our most holy
sins. As there is no-one else to ask,
you start by telling me that sometimes
you pretended to be happy when in fact
you'd have preferred to be unhappily hedonistic —
but that you're proud, still, of the choices you made.
I say I didn't seem to achieve much more than I could,

though I lived amidst unbridled miseries
and abused myself unnecessarily.
After days of this
we are so terrified
we can no longer sit beside each other
or recognise ourselves in the mirror;
we hold the breath in our noses
so that we cannot smell.

There's birdsong right through −
Now I'm consoled by the way you took yourself
out of the room, out of the impossibility −
and left without need for a goodbye kiss,
a souvenir. I wasn't so resourceful.
I attacked everything I saw:
I mutilated the sofas with kitchen knives
when it took you;
I smashed the coffee pot over your photographs;
I kicked and punished the furnishings and the walls
for making our end so commonplace.

When I look at your picture
I think how handsome, how clever
you must be to so compassionately accept
limitations and nature
signing your name
with firm hands.

Edie

The Fair

I've tried hoop-la; I even tried as a grown adult but the pressure
of hanging in for two small kids with open candy-flossed mouths
is *underrated*. Of your two sons, one has pink plastic shoes
and the other's not half as rugged but he's got his bow and arrow:
                                        you —

and I'm your omniscient present, if you will. You're Minnie Mouse.
When you were happy, your tongue was soft in your mouth and
                                        filled
your flesh, which gave gently around your ribcage and lungs. Your
                                        breath
filled your whole body like a field of eucalyptus.

Yes, it is because I desire you honey
that I do not instantly notice that your milk has been dry-sucked,
and you're so hot with the fever of long nights
you need to take off your summer hat, slip off your shoes,

even your t-shirt, maybe your brassiere;
show the circus how those hallucinations tore off the pounds
just by giving you the heebies. Where's the doctor when you need
                                        one,
Edie? He's bobbing for apples to raise money

for people with headaches, teething problems.
You could always try stuffing your belly full of candy
or plugging your uterus with foreign dolls: it works for some.
Or do what other girls do: riddle your synapses with vodka and
                                          don a push-up bra,

make a parade of the million faces you learned well
to travel, to earn and to come home with an appetite
for sexual love that wants to fill the coffee percolator and needs
a thicker duvet in winter and often calls you by made up names.

I know you prefer teddy bears' picnics to plastic fêtes;
all the reinvented kitsch you think innately morose;
that you make soup from stones and hip replacements —
from chewing gum and buttons, bones. A sort of magic that you do,

that smoothing of all the muscles in your body and in your face.
You can do make-up too, take the shadows out and curtly enter
from behind the curtain — look! the boys are singing songs you
                                          taught them
and every inch of the day is a feat of utter maternal professionalism.

When you're sad, I have a bad feeling for you. This I know:
pleasure will just never do. You suffer ecstasy in swathes,
like at the fair where there were carousels that made you go dizzy,
toy guns that made you feel rebellious — sweet stuck painfully

in your cold teeth. But you're home, it's quiet and I'm going
to try and answer some of the questions insomnia

is holding me for. Wish me luck — from your head;
in your wide, soft bed —

when there are no ferris wheels or donkey rides,
and the boys and you are acutely aware of the fear
of being separated; don't concern yourself with the terms
of commitment or the gospels we write ourselves

while in the wings — don't think on why the skin
around your waist feels so pinched, of how and why
you suffer blind and deaf and mute loneliness —
don't bother yourself with reasoning why

you cry out, inaudibly, in pain,
until your husband's sheets are drenched.

Deprivations

To keep alive the wonder of suffering
you have been metamorphosed into me
Anna Ahkmatova

in your father's painting of cornfields I confided
a passion for the colours of your blood

behind your irises there are billions of tears;
your brain is moist as an electrocution sponge —

if you would only permit me, I would tell the world
how scarred your corneas are; how those tears ran

like paint from your father's brushes, like the blood
from your uterus when your waters gave

and your eyelids became dams. How those babies
cried and cried and their cries petrified

the wires that drove electricity through your house;
everywhere you touched you drew sparks,

'til your heart got bruised from the kickbacks.
Please go to sleep now and let go your children's hands —

they will not fly away like crows.

You are so beautiful your tired eyes don't even flinch

at the white word: Sleep.

Rumi

Rumi was our wedding gift from you. A reminder
    of ecstasy; you think me a denouncer of prayer
in favour of blank idols, but I have prayed
    like only a whore knows how.

You're blonde, you have the features of purgatory,
    the feminine blueprint; tragedy has aged your
god and he is earthly. You feel his cold blood
    in the clay, the places your mother implored you

to feel for. You should wear your summer hat —
    don't let your skin burn, your precious skin
is delicate, will peel like a shroud from the body
    of a pharaoh. What brave language

have you made in me, have you freed, succour
    with the alabaster bones of your love and faith;
your blood is the silk that creases in your dressed
    gestures, I know the thing you haven't told.

Secrets do not matter. They are only sugar
    and fat soap. Your soul was Mayan; it was burned
into the flesh of a sleeping child; it was fed
    on the equilibrium of pain and the beauty

of dead sunset. Be careful, it's not your fault

you burn so easily, squirm at rivers, bloated sheep;
the breath of a son in your lap or a buttercup's
gold glowing life in a beam on your throat.

JOE

Rasputin

You're the luckiest   rose
a boy, nude, holding a rose   red
of course, the thorns sticking in
your white palms. You are trying to hide
your belly in my dreams. Even your mother will not
take the rose and put it in a jar
she thinks you're gay   or disturbed
and your dad that you're not his.
Your hair is rabid ginger smoke. (How many
knotted fingers have smoothed it
and dreamed it was breaking   cobweb silk?)
Poets have come to your bed.   I stayed
in Beddgelert once and found a book
in a gift shop with your latest love's
latest elegy *Re: Venus.*

Back of the net, you wrote. If you could
you'd keep your heart
in a pickling jar and make diagrams
of it to explain to whoever it is now
attempts to frustrate you, which part
is devoted to them and which
can never be charged or jump-started.

70 | Melissa Lee-Houghton

There's hardly room for more.
You will need to be sure.
I know, I am a rose.
Imperfect, and not the girl
you once owed. I have roots now,
and you have parole, and culinary skills.

Cradled

my baby is sleeping it was
strange to sleep in your daughter's bed her
room had no curtains and your
woman stoned and rinsing the bottles and teats
and all of us under suspicion
you weren't
anorexic
you were just stubborn you
were too stubborn to faint we had to
sleep on a wood floor curled up like
mice
one girl was called Prairie, an
American student she
returned to the ranch without you the
other was a poet she
took photographs of all her lovers she
had a wall in her room devoted to them you
fucking hated that

There are Only Two Ways to Love

I hope you don't use clean needles
and I hope you do and I hope
somebody cleans up after you and I hope
you have learned to do it yourself.

I hope your grandma hasn't died and I hope
you've stopped taking her money
and I hope you've given something back
since losing your children to bribes and

me. I hope you've written words
and I hope you've written poetry.
I wish someone could graft some of the skin
from my smooth thighs onto the scars we made.

But I wouldn't give you love
and I wouldn't give you money anymore.
I am scrubbed so clean we could
never recognise one another. We could never

meet by accident.
You can't afford the theatre
and you can't afford the emergency room
and you can't afford

to have me tell you what Jung said

or what my mother told me about trust
or what my body told me about love
or what you always told me about liberty.

SELF-PORTRAIT

Interview 5.1

If I may thank god, perdition has already occurred.
I didn't wait for it in a nightdress,
or in shoes too tall that nipped youth in the bud.
I didn't hide my face when it happened,
and the lightbulb didn't splinter.
I saw the edge of a knife glinting, but it may have been
a cheap trick of the light. I didn't wear white;
I wasn't even wearing a coat,
and it was cold beyond grief
though not cold. I wasn't carrying suitcases,
or bearing the sores of a guilty conscience;
I had a young face, and yet my face was old
as my mother's when she stepped out of the shadows
of the attic in winter when I saw her breath.
I wasn't smoking a cigarette.
I didn't reach for the bottle, there wasn't time
to smash a glass, taste blood on my mouth
and understand that blood does not
taste much of death. I wasn't bundled
in a tight knot with an avid love-maker,
my sex always made me different, uninvolved. I didn't smell
like a woman, or a girl. I didn't make it come
with a paintbrush or a pen; I didn't use power tools.

My veins were not flushed with chemicals,
and I was not at the mercy of anything living or dead,
though I believe I was of this world.
I slept with the brain of an insomniac
and suffered diminished responsibility for my inability
to blunt my thoughts or stop writing poems
nobody wanted to read. Yes, I was purely belligerent.
I was in love at the time, but it felt no different
from the love I invested the first time I saw a horse
roll on its back in a wet field like a sappy dog.
Blossom didn't reel around my head
or move in swells around my heels.
Her ghost wasn't waiting, and there were no signs
of forced entry, or that I had been victimised. All
the books in the world lined up, senseless
as tins of processed food, when my mind collapsed
with the great, great weight. I thought that perhaps
I was a witch from another age,
though my heart decried its magic
in favour of love and my love preferred
shaping the bones of the dead until they resembled
the bodies of the living. I admit, I didn't wear a costume,
or any flimsy underwear. Nothing covered
the flaws of my delirious virginity, and I had long since
stopped being seen dead with virgins,
though it took some trouble to avoid them in the street.
I didn't notice that I was filthy with dread, if I was.
There just wasn't time
to fill the tub with water, or anoint my soul

with a blubber flood of tears. It simply doesn't happen that way-
I didn't mean to offend anybody,
though I offended you, myself and, apparently, god.
I swore horribly, I'll admit that.
I forgot about the news stories I had always feared;
I forgot about motorways and pile-ups;
I forgot to wear a seatbelt. Nursery
rhymes occasionally popped into my head,
as if to make light of the situation. I was terrified of dying
with The Grand Old Duke of York
blethering in my head. I didn't use contraceptive devices
and it didn't happen in the catacomb
of my marital bed. Nobody else was watching
because it simply wasn't entertaining. I didn't laugh,
because nothing seemed especially funny.
There were no telegrams or sermons, nobody read me
my rights; I didn't have to sign any papers,
make any sacrifices. I ate nothing, but didn't starve.
I changed my name by deedpole.
I grew breasts, I had sex with women, and teenagers, and men.
I inspired others with orgasms, not books and words.
Some of them put their hands over my mouth,
often innocently. I always
disappointed my parents. My only pleasure
was in making other people happy, or teaching by example
how to make other people live miserably,
but together, at least. I dreamed. I never had much
imagination. All my poetry was the subliminal work of outsiders.
I never attended the demonstration, I never protested

or chained myself to anything but the post of a
bearded man's bed. I did suffer hatred,
though I continue to publicly deny it. I see you don't believe me —
don't worry, I know how this works, I always
understood the art of paradox;
that there are many ways to give away the plot
without telling it at all. I think that's why
we employ psychologists and spiritual healers
to say and do all the really terrible things for us,
and give us faith in what is at best, improbable,
and morbidly useless.
I hate the beating of tides.
I loathe the mooring of boats.
I love the taste of saltwater, and have always been
fascinated by caves, and the glorious reality
of walking among beasts. I will not tell you
what you want to hear unless you bribe me
with emotional gestures or deprive me of sleep
for four days, though I have been known to go for longer.
Please don't tell me you're afraid. I'm not
comfortable with swapping well-defined roles.
There is no firing squad for you or I.
No hangman. No black pillowcase. I will not
ride out of here on horseback, and open fire on my captors,
my greatest allies. I will not make bombs
out of bits of used chewing gum, sherbet and Vaseline
and old record players. I will never manage to thank
the man that digs my grave.
I hope this information

can be of use to the people higher up
when they are making my case. I hate to tell you
but you forgot to turn your Dictaphone on,
and your mouth and hand have not done
anything unutterable for three whole hours. You really
are making me feel very uncomfortable.

Lightning Source UK Ltd.
Milton Keynes UK
UKOW02f1328220616

276843UK00002B/55/P